Vegan Coo
Delicious Vegan
Breakfast, Lunch an
You Can Make in Minutes!

by **Vesela Tabakova**
Text copyright(c)2013 Vesela Tabakova
All Rights Reserved

Table Of Contents

A Cookbook of Creative Vegan Gluten-free Recipes	5
Vegan Gluten-free Salads and Appetizers	6
Greek Chickpea Salad	7
Bulgarian Green Salad	8
Kale Salad with Creamy Tahini Dressing	9
Rocket and Cashew Spread	10
Apple, Celery and Walnut Salad	11
Spinach Stem Salad	12
Fresh Greens Salad	13
Beet and Bean Sprout Salad	14
Spicy Buckwheat Vegetable Salad	15
Mediterranean Buckwheat Salad	16
Buckwheat Salad with Asparagus and Roasted Peppers	18
Roasted Broccoli Buckwheat Salad	20
Garlicky Baby Spinach Salad	21
Winter Cabbage Salad	22
Red Cabbage Salad	23
Okra Salad	24
Fast Cucumber Salad	25
Grated Beetroot Salada	26
Simple Broccoli Salad	27
Carrot and Apple Salad	28
Roasted Eggplant and Pepper Salad	29
Green Bean Salad	30
Haricot Bean Salad	31
Roasted Peppers with Garlic and Parsley	32
Warm Quinoa Salad	33
Minty Quinoa and Black Bean Salad	34
Roasted Vegetable Quinoa Salad	35
Quinoa with Oven Roasted Tomatoes and Vegan Pesto	36
Cucumber Quinoa Salad	38
Fresh Vegetable Quinoa Salad	39
Warm Mushroom Quinoa Salad	40
Quinoa Tabbouleh	41
Quinoa and Asparagus Salad	42

Warm Cauliflower and Quinoa Salad	43
Quinoa, Zucchini and Carrots Salad	44
Vegan Gluten-free Soups	45
Beetroot and Carrot Soup	46
Minty Pea Soup	47
Spiced Citrus Bean Soup	48
Traditional Brown Lentil Soup	49
Moroccan Lentil Soup	50
Lentil and Cabbage Soup	51
Pumpkin and Bell Pepper Soup	52
Spicy Carrot Soup	53
Mushroom Soup	54
Tomato and Quinoa Soup	55
Spinach, Leek and Quinoa Soup	56
Garden Quinoa Soup	57
Spinach and Mushroom Soup	58
Broccoli and Potato Soup	59
Creamy Potato Soup	60
Leek, Rice and Potato Soup	61
Shredded Cabbage Soup	62
Mediterranean Chickpea Soup	63
Carrot and Chickpea Soup	64
Creamy Red Pepper Soup	65
Spring Nettle Soup	66
Gazpacho	67
Avocado Gazpacho	68
Vegan Gluten-free Main Dishes	69
Spinach and Lentil Quinoa Stew	70
Eggplant and Tomato Stew	71
Spicy Eggplant and Chickpea Stew	72
Simple Green Pea Stew	73
Green Pea and Mushroom Stew	74
Grandma's Leek Stew	75
Potato and Leek Stew	76
Zucchini with Rice	77
Spinach with Rice	78

Vegetable Stew	79
Simple Baked Beans	80
Rice Stuffed Bell Peppers	81
Stuffed Red Bell Peppers with Haricot Beans	82
Stuffed Grapevine Leaves	83
Green Bean and Potato Stew	85
Cabbage and Rice Stew	86
Rice with Leeks and Olives	87
Rice and Tomatoes	88
Roasted Cauliflower	89
Stuffed Cabbage Leaves	90
Potato and Zucchini Bake	92
New Potatoes with Herbs	93
Okra and Tomato Casserole	94
Roasted Brussels Sprouts	95
Roasted Butternut Squash	96
Roasted Artichoke Hearts	97
Beet Fries	98
Grilled Vegetable Skewers	99
Vegan Gluten-free Breakfasts and Desserts	100
Quinoa Banana Pudding	101
Raisin Quinoa Breakfast	102
Berry Quinoa Breakfast	103
Baked Apples	104
Pumpkin Baked with Dry Fruit	105
About the Author	106

A Cookbook of Creative Vegan Gluten-free Recipes

Following a vegan gluten-free diet is extremely challenging and often very expensive. Gluten-free foods are hard to find, do not always taste very good and many people who have to avoid gluten feel overwhelmed and depressed by the fact that they have to follow this diet.

The truth is, however, that there is an easy and simple way to stick to a vegan gluten-free diet by focusing on naturally gluten-free whole foods. So much of the food you already love is naturally gluten-free and, therefore, the safest and most nutritious way to follow a gluten-free diet is to cook at home and to stick primarily to fresh, unrefined and unprocessed ingredients. If you want to eat really healthy food with good ingredients, it is best to make it yourself. It's really not that difficult to prepare your meals at home with fresh vegetables, herbs, rice and beans, as well as other naturally gluten-free foods such as my favorite quinoa or buckwheat.

Planning simple, home cooked meals and choosing naturally gluten-free vegan foods should make your transition to a gluten-free lifestyle much easier. Here are some easy-to-make homemade vegan gluten-free recipes to get you cooking.

Vegan Gluten-free Salads and Appetizers

Greek Chickpea Salad

Serves 4

Ingredients:

1 cup canned chickpeas, drained and rinsed

1 spring onion, thinly sliced

1 small cucumber, diced

2 green peppers, diced

2 tomatoes, diced

2 tbsp chopped fresh parsley

1 tsp capers, drained and rinsed

juice of ½ a lemon

2 tsp olive oil

1 tsp balsamic vinegar

salt and pepper, to taste

a pinch of dried oregano

Directions:

In a medium bowl, toss together the chickpeas, spring onion, cucumber, green peppers, tomatoes, parsley, capers and lemon juice.

In a smaller bowl, stir together the remaining ingredients and pour over the chickpea salad.

Toss well to coat and allow to marinate, stirring occasionally, for at least 1 hour before serving.

Bulgarian Green Salad

Serves 4

Ingredients:

1 green lettuce, washed and drained

1 cucumber, sliced

a bunch of radishes, sliced

a bunch of spring onions, finely cut

juice of half lemon or 2 tbsp of white wine vinegar

3 tbsp olive oil

salt to taste

Directions:

Cut the lettuce into thin strips. Slice the cucumber and the radishes as thinly as possible and chop the spring onions.

Mix all the salad ingredients in a large bowl, add the lemon juice and olive oil and season with salt to taste.

Kale Salad with Creamy Tahini Dressing

Serves 4

Ingredients:

1 head kale

2 cucumbers, peeled and diced

1 avocado, peeled and diced

1 red onion, finely chopped

1 cup cherry tomatoes, halved

for the dressing

1/3 cup tahini

1/2 cup water

2 garlic cloves, minced

3 tbsp lemon juice

4 tbsp olive oil

salt and freshly ground black pepper, to taste

Directions:

Prepare the dressing by whisking all ingredients.

Place all salad ingredients in bowl and toss with the dressing.

Season to taste with black pepper and salt.

Rocket and Cashew Spread

Serves: 4

Ingredients:

1 1/2 cup cashews

¼ cup nutritional yeast

2 garlic cloves, chopped

3 cups rocket leaves

5 tbsp olive oil

3 tbsp lemon juice

2 tbsp dill, finely cut

salt, to taste

Directions:

Combine the cashews, nutritional yeast and garlic in a blender and pulse until the ingredients are mixed but the cashews are still chunky. Set aside in a bowl.

Add in the olive oil and lemon juice first, and then the rocket. Pulse to blend well.

Mix rocket mixture into cashew mixture, and season with salt and pepper to taste.

Apple, Celery and Walnut Salad

Serves 4

Ingredients:

3 large apples, quartered, cores removed, thinly sliced

1 celery rib, thinly sliced

½ cup walnuts, chopped

2 tbsp raisins

½ cup sunflower seeds

1 red onion, thinly sliced

3 tbsp apple cider vinegar

2 tbsp olive oil

salt and black pepper, to taste

Directions:

Mix vinegar, olive oil, salt and pepper in a small bowl. Whisk until well combined.

Place apples, celery, onion, walnuts, raisins and sunflower seeds in a bigger salad bowl. Drizzle with dressing and toss gently.

Spinach Stem Salad

Serves 2

Ingredients:

about 9-10 spinach stems

water to boil the stems

2 garlic cloves, crushed

lemon juice or red wine vinegar, to taste

3-4 tbsp olive oil

salt, to taste

Directions:

Trim the stems so that they remain whole and wash them very well. Steam stems in a basket over boiling water for 2-3 minutes, until wilted but not too soft.

Place spinach stems on a plate and sprinkle with crushed garlic, olive oil, lemon juice or vinegar, and salt to taste.

Fresh Greens Salad

Serves 6-7

Ingredients:

1 head red leaf lettuce, rinsed, dried and chopped
1 head green leaf lettuce, rinsed, dried and chopped
1 head endive, rinsed, dried and chopped
1 cup frisee lettuce leaves, rinsed, dried and chopped
3-4 fresh basil leaves, chopped
3-4 fresh mint leaves, chopped
2-3 spring onions, chopped
1 tbsp chia seeds
4 tbsp olive oil
3-4 tbsp lemon juice
1 tsp sugar
salt, to taste

Directions:

Place the red and green leaf lettuce, frisee lettuce, endive, onions, basil and mint into a large salad bowl and toss lightly to combine.

Prepare the dressing from the lemon juice, olive oil and sugar and pour it over the salad. Sprinkle with chia seeds and season with salt to taste.

Beet and Bean Sprout Salad

Serves 4-5

Ingredients:

5-6 beet greens, finely sliced

2 tomatoes, sliced

1 cup bean sprouts, washed

3 tbsp pumpkin seeds

1 tbsp grated lemon rind

2 garlic cloves, crushed

1/3 cup lemon juice

1/3 cup olive oil

1 tsp salt

Directions:

In a large bowl toss together beet greens, bean sprouts, tomatoes and pumpkin seeds.

Mix oil and lemon juice with lemon rind, salt and garlic and pour over the salad. Serve chilled.

Spicy Buckwheat Vegetable Salad

Serves 4-5

Ingredients:

1 cup buckwheat groats

2 cups gluten-free vegetable broth

2 tomatoes, diced

½ cup spring onions, chopped

½ cup parsley leaves, finely chopped

½ cup fresh mint leaves, very finely chopped

½ yellow bell pepper, chopped

1 cucumber, peeled and cut into 1/4-inch cubes

½ cup cooked or canned brown lentils, drained

1/4 cup freshly squeezed lemon juice

1 tsp gluten-free hot pepper sauce

salt, to taste

Directions:

Heat a large, dry saucepan and toast the buckwheat for about three minutes. Boil the vegetable broth and add it carefully to the buckwheat. Cover, reduce heat, and simmer until buckwheat is tender and all liquid is absorbed. Remove from heat, fluff with a fork and set aside to cool.

Chop all vegetables and add them together with the lentils to the buckwheat. Mix the lemon juice and remaining ingredients well and drizzle over the buckwheat mixture. Stir well to distribute the dressing evenly.

Mediterranean Buckwheat Salad

Serves 4-5

Ingredients:

1 cup buckwheat groats

1 3/4 cups water

1 small red onion, finely chopped

½ cucumber, diced

1 cup cherry tomatoes, halved

1 yellow bell pepper, chopped

a bunch of parsley, finely cut

1 preserved lemon, finely chopped

1 cup chickpeas, cooked or canned, drained

juice of half lemon

1 tsp dried basil

2 tbsp olive oil

salt and black pepper, to taste

Directions:

Heat a large dry saucepan and toast the buckwheat for about three minutes. Boil the water and add it carefully to the buckwheat. Cover, reduce heat and simmer until buckwheat is tender and all liquid is absorbed (5-7 minutes). Remove from heat, fluff with a fork and set aside to cool.

Mix the buckwheat with the chopped onion, bell pepper, cucumber, cherry tomatoes, parsley, preserved lemon and chickpeas in a salad bowl.

Whisk the lemon juice with olive oil and basil, season with salt and pepper to taste, pour over the salad and stir. Serve at room temperature.

Buckwheat Salad with Asparagus and Roasted Peppers

Serves 4-5

Ingredients:

1 cup buckwheat groats

1 3/4 cups gluten-free vegetable broth

½ lb asparagus, trimmed and cut into 1 inch pieces

4 roasted red bell peppers, diced

1 tomato, diced

2-3 spring onions, finely chopped

2 garlic cloves, crushed

1 tbsp red wine vinegar

3 tbsp olive oil

salt and black pepper, to taste

½ cup fresh parsley leaves, finely cut

Directions:

Heat a large dry saucepan and toast the buckwheat for about three minutes. Boil the vegetable broth and add it carefully to the buckwheat. Cover, reduce heat and simmer until buckwheat is tender and all liquid is absorbed (5-7 minutes). Remove from heat, fluff with a fork and set aside to cool.

Cook the asparagus in a steamer basket or colander, 2-3 minutes until tender. Transfer it in a large salad bowl along with the roasted peppers and diced tomato. Add in the spring onions, garlic, red wine vinegar, salt, pepper and olive oil. Stir to combine.

Add the buckwheat to the vegetable mixture. Sprinkle with parsley and toss the salad gently. Serve at room temperature.

Roasted Broccoli Buckwheat Salad

Serves 4-5

Ingredients:

1 cup buckwheat groats

1 3/4 cups water

1 head of broccoli, cut into small pieces

1 lb asparagus, trimmed and cut into 1 inch pieces

½ cup roasted cashews

5-4 cup basil leaves, minced

½ cup olive oil

2 garlic cloves, crushed

1 tsp salt

Directions:

Arrange vegetables on a baking sheet and drizzle with olive oil. Roast in a preheated to 350 F oven for about fifteen minutes or until tender.

Heat a large, dry saucepan and toast the buckwheat for about three minutes, or until it releases a nutty aroma. Boil the water and add it carefully to the buckwheat. Cover, reduce heat and simmer until buckwheat is tender and all liquid is absorbed (5-7 minutes). Remove from heat, fluff with a fork and set aside to cool.

Prepare the dressing by blending basil leaves, olive oil, garlic, and salt.

Toss vegetables, buckwheat and dressing together in a salad bowl. Add in cashews and serve.

Garlicky Baby Spinach Salad

Serves 4

Ingredients:

1 bag baby spinach, washed and dried

1 red bell pepper, cut in slices

1 cup cherry tomatoes, cut in halves

1 red onion, finely chopped

1 cup black olives, pitted

1 tsp dried oregano

1 large garlic clove

3 tbsp red wine vinegar

4 tbsp olive oil

salt and freshly ground black pepper, to taste

Directions:

Prepare the dressing by blending the garlic and the oregano with the olive oil and vinegar in a food processor.

Place the spinach leaves in a large salad bowl and toss with the dressing. Add the rest of the ingredients and give everything a toss again. Season to taste with black pepper and salt.

Winter Cabbage Salad

Serves 4

Ingredients:

7 oz fresh white cabbage, shredded

7 oz carrots, shredded

7 oz white turnips, shredded

½ a bunch of parsley

2 tbsp white wine vinegar

3 tbsp sunflower oil

salt, to taste

Directions:

Combine first three ingredients in a large bowl and mix well. Add salt, vinegar and oil.

Stir, sprinkle with parsley and serve.

Red Cabbage Salad

Serves 6

Ingredients:

1 small head red cabbage, cored and chopped

1 bunch of fresh dill, finely cut

3 tbsp sunflower oil

3 tbsp red wine vinegar

1 tsp sugar

2 tsp salt

black pepper to taste

Directions:

In a small bowl, mix the oil, red wine vinegar, sugar and black pepper.

Place the cabbage in a larger glass bowl. Sprinkle the salt on top and crunch it with your hands to soften. Pour dressing over the cabbage and toss to coat.

Sprinkle the salad with dill, cover it with foil and leave it in the refrigerator for half an hour before serving.

Okra Salad

Serves 4

Ingredients:

1.2 lb young okras

1 lemon

½ bunch parsley, chopped

2 tomatoes, sliced

3 tbsp sunflower oil

½ tsp black pepper

salt, to taste

Directions:

Trim okras, then wash and cook them in salted water until tender. Drain and let cool.

In a small bowl, mix well the lemon juice and sunflower oil, salt and black pepper.

Arrange okra and tomatoes in a bowl then pour over the dressing and sprinkle with chopped parsley.

Fast Cucumber Salad

Serves 4

Ingredients:

2 medium cucumbers, peeled and sliced

a bunch of fresh dill, finely cut

2 cloves garlic, minced

3 tbsp white wine vinegar

5 tbsp olive oil

salt, to taste

Directions:

Cut the cucumbers in rings and put them in a salad bowl.

Add the finely cut dill, the pressed garlic, and season with salt, vinegar and oil. Mix well and serve cold.

Grated Beetroot Salad

Serves 4

Ingredients:

2-3 small beets, peeled

3-4 spring onions, cut

3 cloves garlic, minced

2 tbsp red wine vinegar

2-3 tbsp sunflower oil

salt to taste

Directions:

Place the beats in a steam basket set over a pot of boiling water. Steam for about 12-15 minutes, or until tender. Leave to cool.

Grate the beets and put them in a salad bowl. Add the crushed garlic cloves, the finely cut spring onions and mix well.

Season with salt, vinegar and sunflower oil.

Simple Broccoli Salad

Serves 4

Ingredients:

14 oz fresh broccoli, cut into florets

3-4 fresh onions, finely cut

1/3 cup raisins

1/3 cup sunflower seeds

1 garlic clove, crushed

1/4 cup orange juice

3 tbsp olive oil

Directions:

Combine broccoli, onions, raisins, and sunflower seeds in a medium salad bowl.

In a smaller bowl whisk the orange juice, garlic and olive oil until blended. Pour over the broccoli mixture and toss to coat.

Carrot and Apple Salad

Serves 4

Ingredients:

4 carrots, shredded

1 apple, peeled, cored and shredded

2 garlic cloves, crushed

2 tbsp lemon juice

salt and pepper, to taste

Directions:

In a salad bowl, combine the shredded carrots, apple, lemon juice, garlic, salt and pepper.

Toss and chill before serving.

Roasted Eggplant and Pepper Salad

Serves 4

Ingredients:

2 medium eggplants

2 red or green bell peppers

2 tomatoes

3 cloves garlic, crushed

fresh parsley

1-2 tbsp red wine vinegar

olive oil, as needed

salt, pepper

Directions:

Wash and dry the vegetables. Prick the skin off the eggplants. Bake the eggplants, tomatoes and peppers in a preheated oven at 480 F, for about 40 minutes, or until the skins are well burnt.

Take out of the oven and leave in a covered container for about 10 minutes. Peel the skins off and drain well the extra juices. De-seed the peppers.

Cut all the vegetables into small pieces. Add the garlic and mix well with a fork or in a food processor. Add the olive oil, vinegar and salt to taste. Stir again.

Serve cold and sprinkled with parsley.

Green Bean Salad

Serves 6

Ingredients:

2 cups green beans, cooked

1 onion, sliced

4 garlic cloves, crushed

3-4 fresh mint leaves, chopped

1 bunch of fresh dill, finely chopped

3 tbsp olive oil

1 tbsp apple cider vinegar

salt and pepper, to taste

Directions:

Put the green beans in a medium bowl and mix with onion, mint and dill.

In a smaller bowl, stir olive oil, vinegar, garlic, salt and pepper. Toss into the green bean mixture.

Haricot Bean Salad

Serves 4-5

Ingredients:

1 cup haricot beans

1 onion, cut

3 tbsp white wine vinegar

1 bunch of fresh parsley

salt and black pepper

Directions:

Wash the beans and soak them in cold water to swell overnight. Cook in the same water with the peeled onion. When tender, drain and put into a deeper bowl. Remove the onion.

Mix well oil, vinegar, salt and pepper. Pour over the still warm beans, leave to cool about 30-40 minutes.

Chop the onion and the parsley, add to the beans, mix and leave to cool for at least 40 minutes. Serve cold.

Roasted Peppers with Garlic and Parsley

Serves 4-6

Ingredients:

2.25 lb red and green bell peppers

½ cup sunflower oil

1/3 cup white wine vinegar

3-4 cloves garlic, chopped

a bunch of fresh parsley

salt and pepper, to taste

Directions:

Grill the peppers or roast them in the oven at 480 F until the skins are a little burnt. Place the roasted peppers in a brown paper bag or a lidded container and leave covered for about 10 minutes. This makes it easier to peel them.

Peel the skins and remove the seeds. Cut the peppers into 1 inch strips lengthwise and layer them in a bowl.

Mix together the oil, vinegar, salt and pepper, chopped garlic and chopped parsley leaves. Pour over the peppers.

Cover the roasted peppers and chill for an hour.

Warm Quinoa Salad

Serves 6

Ingredients:

1 cup quinoa

½ cup green beans, frozen

½ cup sweet corn, frozen

½ cup carrots, diced

½ cup black olives, pitted and halved

2-3 garlic cloves, crushed

2 tbsp fresh dill, finely cut

3 tbsp lemon juice

2 tbsp olive oil

Directions:

Wash quinoa with lots of water. Strain it and cook it according to package directions. When ready, set aside in a large salad bowl and fluff with a fork.

Heat olive oil in a large saucepan over medium heat. Stew green beans, sweet corn, olives and carrots until vegetables are tender.

Add this mixture to quinoa and stir to combine.

In a smaller bowl, combine lemon juice, dill and garlic and pour over the warm salad. Add salt and black pepper to taste and serve.

Minty Quinoa and Black Bean Salad

Serves 6

Ingredients:

1 cup quinoa

1 cup black beans, cooked, rinsed and drained

½ cup sweet corn, cooked

1 red bell pepper, deseeded and chopped

4-5 spring onions, chopped

2 garlic cloves, crushed

1 tbsp dry mint

3 tbsp lemon juice

½ tsp salt

4 tbsp olive oil

Directions:

Rinse quinoa in a fine sieve under cold running water until water runs clear. Put quinoa in a pot with two cups of water. Bring to a boil, then reduce heat, cover and simmer for fifteen minutes or until water is absorbed and quinoa is tender. Fluff quinoa with a fork and set aside to cool.

Put beans, corn, bell pepper, spring onions and garlic in a salad bowl and toss to combine. Add quinoa and toss well again.

In a smaller bowl whisk together lemon juice, salt and olive oil and drizzle over salad. Toss well and serve.

Roasted Vegetable Quinoa Salad

Serves 6

Ingredients:

2 zucchinis, cut into bite sized pieces

1 eggplant, peeled and cut into bite sized pieces

3 roasted red peppers, peeled cut into bite sized pieces

4-5 small white mushrooms, whole

1 cup quinoa

½ cup olive oil

2 tbsp apple cider vinegar

1 tsp summer savory

salt and pepper, to taste

Directions:

Toss the zucchinis, mushrooms and eggplant in half the olive oil, salt and black pepper. Place on a baking sheet in a single layer and bake in a preheated 350 F oven for 30 minutes flipping once.

Wash well, strain, and cook quinoa following package directions.

Prepare the dressing from the remaining olive oil, apple cider vinegar, summer savory, salt and black pepper. In a big bowl combine quinoa, roasted zucchinis, eggplant, mushrooms and roasted red peppers. Toss the dressing into the salad.

Quinoa with Oven Roasted Tomatoes and Vegan Pesto

Serves 6

Ingredients :

1 cup quinoa

2 cups water

1 cup cherry tomatoes, for roasting

½ cup cherry tomatoes, fresh

1 avocado, cut into chunks

½ cup black olives, pitted

for the pesto

2 cloves garlic, chopped

½ tsp salt

½ cup walnuts, toasted

1 cup basil leaves

1 tbsp lemon juice

4-6 tbsp olive oil

1 tsp summer savory

2 tbsp water (optional)

Directions:

Preheat the oven to 350 F and line a baking sheet with foil or baking paper. Wash and dry a cup of cherry tomatoes, arrange them on the baking sheet, drizzle with olive oil and savory and toss to coat well.

Bake the tomatoes for about twenty minutes, flipping once, until they are brown. Sprinkle with salt.

Rinse quinoa very well in a fine mesh strainer under running water; set aside to drain. Place two cups of water and quinoa in a large saucepan over medium-high heat. Bring to the boil, then reduce heat to low. Simmer for fifteen minutes. Set quinoa aside, covered, for ten minutes and fluff with a fork.

Make the homemade pesto by placing garlic, walnuts and ½ teaspoon of salt in a food processor. Add basil and lemon juice and blend in batches until smooth. Add oil, one tablespoon at a time, processing in between, until the pesto is light and creamy. Taste for salt and add more if you like.

In a large mixing bowl, gently mix the quinoa with the tomatoes, avocado and olives. Spoon in the pesto and toss to distribute it evenly.

Cucumber Quinoa Salad

Serves 6

Ingredients:

1 cup quinoa

2 cups water

1 large cucumber, diced

½ cup black olives, pitted

2 tbsp lemon juice

2 tbsp olive oil

1 bunch fresh dill, finely cut

Directions:

Wash quinoa very well in a fine mesh strainer under running water and set aside to drain. Place quinoa and two cups of cold water in a saucepan over high heat and bring to the boil. Reduce heat to low and simmer for fifteen minutes. Set aside, covered, for ten minutes, then transfer to a large bowl.

Add the finely cut dill, diced cucumber and olives and toss to combine.

Prepare a dressing from the lemon juice, olive oil, salt and pepper. Add it to the salad and toss to combine.

Fresh Vegetable Quinoa Salad

Serves 6

Ingredients:

1 cup quinoa

2 cups water

a bunch of spring onions, chopped

2 green peppers, chopped

½ cup black olives, pitted and chopped

2 tomatoes, diced

1 cup sunflower seeds

3 tbsp olive oil

4 tbsp fresh lemon juice

1 tbsp dried mint

Directions:

Prepare the dressing by combining olive oil, lemon juice and dried mint in a small bowl and mixing it well. Place the dressing in the refrigerator until ready to use.

Wash well and cook quinoa according to package directions. When it is ready leave it aside for ten minutes, then transfer it to a large bowl.

Add the diced peppers, finely cut spring onions, olives and diced tomatoes, stirring until mixed well.

Stir the dressing and add it to the salad, tossing to evenly coat. Add salt and pepper to taste and sprinkle with sunflower seeds.

Warm Mushroom Quinoa Salad

Serves 4-5

Ingredients:

1 cup quinoa

2 cups gluten-free vegetable broth

1 tbsp sunflower oil

2-3 spring onions, chopped

2 garlic cloves, chopped

10 white mushrooms, sliced

1-2 springs of fresh rosemary

½ cup dried tomatoes, chopped

2 tbsp olive oil

salt and freshly ground black pepper

½ bunch fresh parsley, finely cut

Directions:

Wash well the quinoa in plenty of cold water, strain it and put it in a saucepan. Add vegetable broth and bring to the boil. Lower heat and simmer for ten minutes until the broth is absorbed.

Heat oil in a frying pan and sauté onions for 2-3 minutes. Add garlic and sauté for another minute. Add sliced mushrooms and season with salt and pepper. Add the rosemary and cook the mushrooms until soft.

Combine quinoa with mushrooms and dried tomatoes. Serve sprinkled with fresh parsley.

Quinoa Tabbouleh

Serves 6

Ingredients:

1 cup quinoa

2 cups water

2 cups parsley leaves, finely cut

2 tomatoes, chopped

3 tbsp olive oil

2 garlic cloves, minced

6-7 spring onions, chopped

2-3 tbsp fresh mint leaves, chopped

juice of two lemons

salt and black pepper, to taste

Directions:

Rinse quinoa very well in a fine mesh strainer under running water; set aside to drain. Place water and quinoa in a large saucepan over medium-high heat. Bring to the boil, then reduce heat to low. Simmer for 15 minutes. Set aside, covered, for 10 minutes.

In a salad bowl, mix together the finely cut parsley, tomatoes, olive oil, garlic, spring onions and mint. Stir in the already chilled quinoa and season to taste with salt, pepper, and lemon juice.

Quinoa and Asparagus Salad

Serves 6

Ingredients:

1 cup quinoa

2 cups water

10-11 asparagus stalks, woody ends trimmed, cut

2 bell peppers, deseeded, chopped

¼ cup sunflower seeds

4 spring onions, chopped

2 tbsp fresh parsley, finely cut

2 tbsp lemon juice

1 tsp sugar

2 tbsp olive oil

1 tsp paprika

Directions:

Rinse quinoa very well in a fine mesh strainer under running water; set aside to drain. Place water and quinoa in a large saucepan over medium-high heat. Bring to the boil then reduce heat to low. Simmer for 15 minutes or until just tender. Set aside, covered, for 10 minutes.

Preheat an electric grill or grill pan and cook the asparagus for 2-3 minutes, or until tender crisp. Combine the asparagus, bell pepper, sunflower seeds, spring onions and parsley with the quinoa.

Whisk the lemon juice, sugar, oil and paprika in a small bowl until well combined. Add the dressing to the quinoa mixture. Season with black pepper and toss to combine.

Warm Cauliflower and Quinoa Salad

Serves 4

Ingredients:

1 small cauliflower, cut into florets

1 cup quinoa

2 cups water

1 tbsp paprika

salt, to taste

½ bunch spring onions, finely cut

5-6 tbsp olive oil

Directions:

Preheat oven to 350 F. Cut the cauliflower into bite sized pieces and place it in a roasting dish. Toss in olive oil, salt and paprika and roast, stirring occasionally until golden on the edges and soft.

Wash quinoa well and place in a medium saucepan with two cups of water. Simmer for 15 minutes then set aside for 3-4 minutes.

Serve quinoa topped with cauliflower and sprinkled with spring onions.

Quinoa, Zucchini and Carrots Salad

Serves 6

Ingredients:

1 cup quinoa

2 cups water

2 big carrots, sliced lengthwise into thin ribbons

1 zucchini, sliced lengthwise into thin ribbons

1 big cucumber, sliced lengthwise into thin ribbons

2 garlic cloves, minced

2 tbsp orange juice

1 tbsp apple cider vinegar

2 tbsp olive oil

black pepper, to taste

Directions:

Rinse the quinoa very well in a fine mesh strainer under running water; set aside to drain. Place water and quinoa in a large saucepan over medium-high heat. Bring to the boil then reduce heat to low. Simmer for 15 minutes or until just tender. Set aside, covered for 10 minutes.

Peel lengthwise the carrots and zucchini into thin ribbons. Steam them for 3-4 minutes. Peel the cucumber into ribbons too.

Prepare a dressing by mixing the orange juice, vinegar, olive oil and minced garlic.

Serve quinoa on each plate and arrange some of the vegetable stripes over it. Top with 2-3 tablespoons of the dressing.

Vegan Gluten-free Soups

Beetroot and Carrot Soup

Serves 6

Ingredients:

4 beets, washed and peeled

2 carrots, peeled, chopped

2 potatoes, peeled, chopped

1 medium onion, chopped

2 cups gluten-free vegetable broth

3 cups water

2 tbsp olive oil

a bunch or spring onions, chopped, to serve

Directions:

Peel and chop the beets. Heat olive oil in a saucepan over medium high heat and sauté the onion and carrot until onion is tender. Add beets, potatoes, broth and water. Bring to the boil. Reduce heat to medium and simmer, partially covered, for 30-40 minutes, or until beets are tender. Cool slightly.

Blend soup in batches until smooth. Return it to pan over low heat and cook, stirring, for 4-5 minutes or until heated through.

Season with salt and pepper and serve sprinkled with spring onions.

Minty Pea Soup

Serves 4

Ingredients:

1 onion, finely chopped

2 garlic cloves, finely chopped

4 cups gluten-free vegetable broth

1/3 cup mint leaves

2 lb green peas, frozen

3 tbsp olive oil

5-6 mint leaves, to serve

Directions:

Heat oil in a large saucepan over medium-high heat and sauté onion and garlic for 5 minutes or until soft.

Add gluten-free vegetable broth and bring to the boil, then add mint and peas. Cover, reduce heat, and cook for 3 minutes, or until peas are tender but still green.

Remove from heat. Set aside to cool slightly, then blend in batches, until smooth.

Return soup to saucepan over medium-low heat and cook until heated through. Season with salt and pepper and serve topped with black pepper and mint leaves.

Spiced Citrus Bean Soup

Serves 6-7

Ingredients:

1 can (14 oz) white beans, rinsed and drained

2 medium carrots, cut

1 medium onion, chopped

1 tbsp garam masala

4 cups gluten-free vegetable broth

1 cup coconut milk

1/2 tbsp grated ginger

juice of 1 orange

salt and pepper, to taste

1/2 cup fresh parsley leaves, finely cut, to serve

Directions:

In a large soup pot, sauté onions, carrots and ginger in olive oil, for about 5 minutes, stirring. Add gram masala and cook until just fragrant.

Add the orange juice and vegetable broth and bring to the boil. Simmer for about 10 min until the carrots are tender, then stir in the coconut milk.

Blend soup to desired consistency then add the beans and bring to a simmer. Serve sprinkled with parsley.

Traditional Brown Lentil Soup

Serves 7-8

Ingredients:

1 ½ cups brown lentils

2 onions, chopped

5-6 cloves garlic, peeled

2 medium carrots, chopped

1-2 medium tomatoes, ripe

7-8 cups of water

4 tbsp olive oil

1 tbsp paprika

1 tbsp summer savory or oregano

Directions:

Heat the oil in a cooking pot, add the onions, carrots and garlic and sauté until golden. Add the paprika and washed lentils and stir. Add in water, bring to the boil then lower heat and simmer for 20 minutes.

Chop the tomatoes and add them to the soup, then cook 15 more minutes. Add savory, stir and serve hot.

Moroccan Lentil Soup

Serves 7-8

Ingredients:

1 cup red lentils

½ cup canned chickpeas, drained

2 onions, chopped

2 cloves garlic, minced

1 cup canned tomatoes, chopped

½ cup canned white beans, drained

3 carrots, diced

3 celery ribs, diced

6-7 cups water

1 tsp ginger, grated

1 tsp ground cardamom

½ tsp ground cumin

3 tbsp olive oil

Directions:

In a large pot, sauté onions, garlic and ginger in olive oil, for about 5 minutes. Add the water, lentils, chickpeas, white beans, tomatoes, carrots, celery, cardamom and cumin.

Bring to a boil for a few minutes, then simmer for ½ hour or longer, until the lentils are tender. Puree half the soup in a food processor or blender. Return the pureed soup to the pot, stir and serve.

Lentil and Cabbage Soup

Serves 6-7

Ingredients:

1 cup brown lentils

½ onion, finely cut

2 carrots, cut

1 celery rib, chopped

½ head cabbage, sliced

2 garlic cloves, crushed

3 cups gluten-free vegetable broth

1 cup water

2 tbsp olive oil

1 tbsp summer savory

1 tbsp paprika

salt and pepper, to taste

Directions:

In a large soup pot, heat olive oil over medium-high heat and gently sauté onion and garlic for a minute or two. Add in celery, carrots and cook for an addition 2 minutes.

Once the onion is tender add paprika, savory, dry lentils and stir well. Stir in 3 cups of vegetable broth, and 1 cup water.

Bring soup to a boil, add cabbage, lower heat, and simmer for about 30-40 minutes, or until the cabbage is tender.

Pumpkin and Bell Pepper Soup

Serves 4

Ingredients:

1 medium leek, chopped

9 oz pumpkin, peeled, deseeded, cut into small cubes

½ red bell pepper, cut into small pieces

1 can tomatoes, undrained, crushed

2 cups gluten-free vegetable broth

1-2 cups water

½ tsp ground cumin

salt and black pepper, to taste

Directions:

Heat the olive oil in a medium saucepan and sauté the leek for 4-5 minutes. Add the pumpkin and bell pepper and cook, stirring, for 2-3 minutes. Add tomatoes, broth, water and cumin and bring to the boil.

Cover, reduce heat to low and simmer, stirring occasionally, for 30 minutes, or until vegetables are soft. Season with salt and pepper and leave aside to cool.

Blend in batches and re-heat to serve.

Spicy Carrot Soup

Serves 6-8

Ingredients:

10 carrots, peeled and chopped

2 medium onions, chopped

4-5 cups water

5 tbsp coconut oil

2 cloves garlic, minced

1 red chili pepper, finely chopped

½ bunch, fresh coriander, finely cut

salt and pepper, to taste

Directions:

Heat the coconut oil in a large pot over medium heat, and sauté the onions, carrots, garlic and chili pepper until tender. Add 4-5 cups of water and bring to a boil. Reduce heat to low and simmer 30 minutes.

Transfer the soup to a blender or food processor and blend until smooth. Return to the pot and continue cooking for a few more minutes.

Remove soup from heat, and set aside. Serve with coriander sprinkled over each serving.

Mushroom Soup

Serves 4

Ingredients:

2 cups mushrooms, peeled and chopped

1 onion, chopped

2 cloves of garlic, crushed and chopped

1 tsp dried thyme

2 cups gluten-free vegetable broth

1 cup water

salt and pepper, to taste

3 tbsp olive oil

Directions:

Sauté onions and garlic in a large soup pot until transparent. Add thyme and mushrooms.

Cook, stirring, for 10 minutes then add vegetable broth, water, and simmer for another 10-20 minutes. Blend, season and serve.

Tomato and Quinoa Soup

Serves 4

Ingredients:

4 cups chopped fresh tomatoes or 2 cups canned tomatoes

1 large onion, diced

1/3 cup quinoa, washed very well

2 cups water

4 garlic cloves, minced

3 tbsp olive oil

1 tsp salt

½ tsp black pepper

½ tbsp sugar

½ bunch of fresh parsley

Directions:

Sauté onions and garlic in oil in a large soup pot. When onions have softened, add tomatoes and water and bring to a boil.

Lower heat and simmer for 5 minutes. Blend the soup then return to the pot.

Stir in quinoa and sugar and bring to a boil again, then reduce heat and simmer 15 minutes, stirring occasionally. Sprinkle with parsley and serve.

Spinach, Leek and Quinoa Soup

Serves 6

Ingredients:

½ cup quinoa, very well washed

2 leeks halved lengthwise and sliced

1 onion, chopped

2 garlic cloves, chopped

2 tbsp olive oil

1 can diced tomatoes, (15 oz), undrained

2 cups fresh spinach, cut

4 cups gluten-free vegetable broth

salt and pepper, to taste

Directions:

Heat olive oil in a large pot over medium heat and sauté onion for 2 minutes, stirring. Add leeks and cook for another 2-3 minutes, then add garlic and stir. Season with salt and black pepper to taste.

Add the vegetable broth, canned tomatoes and quinoa. Bring to a boil then reduce heat and simmer for 10 minutes. Stir in spinach and cook for another 5 minutes.

Garden Quinoa Soup

Serves 6

Ingredients:

½ cup quinoa

1 onion, chopped

1 potato, diced

1 carrot, diced

1 red bell pepper, chopped

2 tomatoes, chopped

1 small zucchini, diced

1 tsp dried oregano

3-4 tbsp olive oil

black pepper, to taste

4 cups water

2 tbsp fresh lemon juice

Directions:

Rinse quinoa very well in a fine mesh strainer under running water; set aside to drain.

Heat the oil in a large soup pot and gently sauté the onions and carrot for 2-3 minutes, stirring every now and then. Add in the potato, bell pepper, tomatoes, spices and water. Stir to combine.

Cover, bring to a boil, then lower heat and simmer for 10 minutes.

Add in the quinoa and the zucchini; cover and simmer for 15 minutes or until the vegetables are tender. Add in the lemon juice; stir to combine.

Spinach and Mushroom Soup

Serves 4-5

Ingredients:

1 small onion, finely cut

1 small carrot, chopped

1 small zucchini, diced

2 medium potatoes, diced

5-6 white mushrooms, chopped

2 cups chopped fresh spinach

4 cups gluten-free vegetable broth or water

4 tbsp olive oil

salt and black pepper, to taste

Directions:

Heat olive oil in a large pot over medium heat. Add potatoes, onions and mushroom and cook until vegetables are soft but not mushy.

Add the chopped fresh spinach, zucchini, vegetable broth and simmer for about 20 minutes. Season to taste with salt and pepper.

Broccoli and Potato Soup

Serves 6

Ingredients:

2 lbs broccoli, cut into florets

2 potatoes, chopped

1 big onion, chopped

3 garlic cloves, crushed

4 cups water

1 tbsp olive oil

¼ tsp ground nutmeg

Directions:

Heat oil in a large saucepan over medium-high heat. Add onion and garlic and sauté, stirring, for 3 minutes, or until soft.

Add broccoli, potato and 4 cups of cold water. Cover, and bring to the boil, then reduce heat to low. Simmer, stirring, for 10-15 minutes, or until potatoes are is tender. Remove from heat. Blend until smooth.

Return to pan. Cook for 5 minutes or until heated through. Season with nutmeg and black pepper before serving.

Creamy Potato Soup

Serves 6-7

Ingredients:

4-5 medium potatoes, cut into small cubes

2 carrots, chopped

1 zucchini, chopped

1 celery rib, chopped

5 cups water

3 tbsp olive oil

½ tsp dried rosemary

salt to taste

black pepper to taste

a bunch of fresh parsley for garnish, finely cut

Directions:

Heat the olive oil over medium heat and sauté the vegetables for 2-3 minutes. Pour 4 cups of water, add the rosemary and bring the soup to a boil, then lower heat and simmer until all the vegetables are tender.

Blend soup in a blender until smooth. Serve warm, seasoned with black pepper and parsley sprinkled over each serving.

Leek, Rice and Potato Soup

Serves 6

Ingredients:

2-3 potatoes, diced

1 small onion, chopped

1 leek halved lengthwise and sliced

1/3 cup rice

5 cups of water

3 tbsp olive oil

lemon juice, to serve

Directions:

Heat a soup pot over medium heat. Add olive oil and sauté onion for 2 minutes. Add leeks and potatoes and cook for a few minutes more.

Add water, bring the soup to a boil then reduce heat and simmer for 5 minutes. Add the very well washed rice and simmer for 10 more minutes.

Serve with lemon juice to taste.

Shredded Cabbage Soup

Serves 4-5

Ingredients:

1 large onion, finely chopped

3 tbsp sunflower oil

2 cups gluten-free vegetable broth

1 small cabbage, shredded

1 carrot, sliced

1 medium potato, diced

1 celery rib, sliced

2 tomatoes, diced

½ tsp cumin

salt, to taste

black pepper, to taste

Directions:

Heat the sunflower oil over medium heat and gently sauté the onion for 2-3 minutes. Add cabbage and stir; add in carrots, potatoes, celery, tomatoes and cumin and stir again.

Add in in the broth and enough water to thoroughly cover all ingredients. Bring the soup to a boil, reduce heat and simmer for 1 hour. Season with salt and black pepper to taste.

Mediterranean Chickpea Soup

Serves 7-8

Ingredients:

2 cups canned chickpeas, drained

a bunch of green onions, finely cut

2 cloves garlic, crushed

1 cup canned tomatoes, diced

6 cups gluten-free vegetable broth

3 tbsp olive oil

1 bay leaf

½ tsp crushed rosemary

Directions:

Sauté onion and garlic in olive oil in a heavy soup pot. Add broth, chickpeas, tomato, bay leaf, and rosemary.

Bring to the boil, then reduce heath and simmer for 30 minutes. Remove from heat and serve.

Carrot and Chickpea Soup

Serves 4-5

Ingredients:

3-4 big carrots, chopped

1 leek, chopped

4 cups gluten-free vegetable broth

1 cup canned chickpeas, undrained

½ cup orange juice

2 tbsp olive oil

½ tsp cumin

½ tsp ginger

Directions:

Heat oil in a large saucepan over medium heat. Add leek and carrots and sauté until soft. Add orange juice, broth, chickpeas and spices.

Bring to the boil then reduce heat to medium-low and simmer, covered, for 15 minutes.

Blend soup until smooth; return to pan. Season with salt and pepper. Stir over heat until heated through.

Creamy Red Pepper Soup

Serves 4

Ingredients:

5-6 red peppers

1 large onion, chopped

2 garlic cloves, crushed

4 medium tomatoes, chopped

2 cups gluten-free vegetable broth

3 tbsp olive oil

2 bay leaves

Directions:

Grill the peppers or roast them in the oven at 480 F until the skins are a little burnt. Place the roasted peppers in a brown paper bag or a lidded container and leave covered for about 10 minutes. This makes it easier to peel them. Peel the skins and remove the seeds. Cut the peppers in small pieces.

Heat oil in a large saucepan over medium-high heat. Add onion and garlic and sauté, stirring, for 3 minutes or until onion has softened. Add the red peppers, bay leaves, tomato and simmer for 5 minutes.

Add broth and season with black pepper. Bring to the boil, then reduce heat and simmer for 20 minutes. Set aside to cool slightly. Blend, in batches, until smooth and serve.

Spring Nettle Soup

Serves 4-5

Ingredients:

1.5 lb young top shoots of nettles, well washed

1 cup spinach leaves

1 carrot, chopped

a bunch of spring onions, coarsely chopped

3 tbsp sunflower oil

3 cups hot water

1 tsp salt

Directions:

Clean the young nettles, wash and cook them in slightly salted water. Drain, rinse, drain again and then chop or pass through a sieve.

Sauté the chopped spring onions and carrot in the oil until the onion softens. Add the nettles, the spinach leaves and gradually stir in the water. Bring to a boil, reduce heat and simmer for 5 minutes.

Set aside to cool then blend in batches.

Gazpacho

Serves 5-6

Ingredients:

6-7 medium tomatoes, peeled and halved

1 onion, sliced

1 green pepper, sliced

1 big cucumber, peeled and sliced

2 cloves garlic

salt to taste

4 tbsp olive oil

to garnish

½ onion, chopped

1 green pepper, chopped

1 cucumber, chopped

Directions:

Place the tomatoes, garlic, onion, green pepper, cucumber, salt and olive oil in a blender or food processor and puree until smooth, adding small amounts of cold water if needed to achieve desired consistency.

Serve the gazpacho chilled with the chopped onion, green pepper and cucumber.

Avocado Gazpacho

Serves 4

Ingredients:

2 ripe avocados, peeled, pitted and diced

1 cup tomatoes, diced

1 cup cucumbers, peeled and diced

1 small onion, chopped

2 tbsp lemon juice

1 tsp salt

black pepper, to taste

Directions:

Place avocados, cucumbers, tomatoes, onion, lemon juice and salt and pepper in a blender.

Blend until smooth and serve sprinkled with cilantro or parsley leaves.

Vegan Gluten-free Main Dishes

Spinach and Lentil Quinoa Stew

Serves 6

Ingredients:

½ cup brown lentils

½ cup quinoa

3 cups fresh spinach or about half package of frozen spinach, thawed

1 onion, chopped

2 medium carrots, chopped

2 cloves garlic, cut

3 tbsp olive oil

1 tbsp paprika

2 tsp summer savory

2 cups water

salt and black pepper, to taste

Directions:

Heath the olive oil in a big pot and sauté the onion and carrots for 4-5 minutes. Add garlic, paprika, savory and lentils and sauté for a minute while stirring.

Add the water, bring to a boil, lower the heat and cook for 15 minutes. Wash and rinse the quinoa and add it to the pot with salt and pepper to taste.

Stir well and bring to the boil then lower heat and simmer for 10 minutes. Cut the spinach and add it to the pot. Cook for 4-5 more minutes.

Eggplant and Tomato Stew

Serves 4

Ingredients:

2 medium eggplants, peeled and diced

1 cup canned tomatoes, drained and diced

1 zucchini, diced

9-10 black olives, pitted

1 onion, chopped

4 garlic cloves, chopped

2 tbsp tomato paste

1 cup canned tomatoes, drained and diced

1 bunch of parsley, chopped, to serve

3 tbsp olive oil

1 tbsp paprika

salt and black pepper, to taste

Directions:

Gently sauté onions, garlic, and eggplants in olive oil on medium-high heat for 10 minutes. Add paprika and tomato paste and sauté, stirring, for 1-2 minutes. Add in the rest of the ingredients.

Cover and simmer on low-heat for 30-40 minutes. Sprinkle with parsley and serve.

Spicy Eggplant and Chickpea Stew

Serves 4

Ingredients:

2-3 eggplants, peeled and diced

1 onion, chopped

2-3 garlic cloves, crushed

1 (15 oz) can chickpeas, drained

1 (15 oz) can tomatoes, undrained, diced

1 tsp paprika

½ tsp cinnamon

1 tsp cumin

4 tbsp olive oil

salt and pepper, to taste

Directions:

Peel and dice the eggplants. Heat olive oil in a large deep frying pan and sauté onions and crushed garlic. Add paprika, cumin and cinnamon. Stir well to coat evenly.

Sauté for 3-4 minutes until the onions have softened. Add the eggplant, tomatoes and chickpeas. Bring to a boil, lower heat and simmer, covered, for 15 minutes, or until the eggplant is tender.

Uncover and simmer for a few more minutes until the liquid evaporates.

Simple Green Pea Stew

Serves 5

Ingredients:

2 cups green peas from a can, drained

1 medium onion, finely cut

2 carrots, chopped

4 tbsp sunflower oil

1 tsp paprika

½ bunch of fresh dill, finely cut

4 cloves garlic

salt, to taste

Directions:

Sauté the finely chopped onion and carrots. Add garlic, paprika and green peas and simmer with some warm water for 20 minutes.

Season with salt and black pepper to taste. When ready sprinkle with finely cut dill.

Green Pea and Mushroom Stew

Serves 4

Ingredients:

1 cup green peas (fresh or frozen)

4 large mushrooms, sliced

3 spring onions, chopped

1-2 cloves garlic

4 tbsp olive oil

½ cup water

½ bunch of finely chopped dill

Directions:

In a saucepan sauté mushrooms, green onions and garlic. Add green peas and stew for 5-10 minutes until tender.

Sprinkle with dill and serve.

Grandma's Leek Stew

Serves 4

Ingredients:

1 lb leeks, cut

4 tbsp sunflower oil

½ cup gluten-free vegetable broth

2 tbsp tomato paste

salt, to taste

fresh ground pepper, to taste

Directions:

Carefully clean the leeks; cutting off the stemmy bottoms and the dark green leaves. Cut the remaining white parts lengthwise in quarters, then into about 1 inch squares.

Heat oil in a heavy wide saucepan or sauté pan; add leeks, salt, pepper, and stir over low heat for 5 minutes. Add vegetable broth and bring to a boil.

Cover and simmer over low heat, stirring often, for about 10-15 minutes or until leeks are tender. Add tomato paste, raise heat to medium, uncover and let the juices reduce to about half.

Potato and Leek Stew

Serves 4

Ingredients:

4-5 potatoes, peeled and diced

2-3 leek stems cut into thick rings

5-6 tbsp olive oil

½ bunch of parsley

salt, to taste

Directions:

Peel the potatoes, wash them and cut them into small cubes. Slice the leeks. Put the potatoes and the leeks in a pot along with some water and the oil. The water should cover the vegetables.

Season with salt and bring to the boil, then simmer until tender. Sprinkle with the finely chopped parsley.

Zucchini with Rice

Serves 4

Ingredients:

4 zucchinis, diced

1 bunch spring onions, finely chopped

5 tbsp sunflower oil

2 cups water

2 medium tomatoes, diced

1 cup rice

1/2 tsp salt

1 tbsp paprika

1/2 tsp black pepper

1 bunch fresh dill, finely cut

Directions:

Sauté green onions in oil and a little water. Cover and cook until soft.

Transfer onions in a baking dish, add zucchinis, tomatoes, rice, salt, paprika, pepper and water. Mix well. Cover with foil and bake in preheated to 350 F oven for 30 minutes, or until rice is done.

Sprinkle with fresh dill and serve.

Spinach with Rice

Serves 4

Ingredients:

1.5 lb fresh spinach, washed, drained and chopped

½ cup rice

1 onion, chopped

1 carrot, chopped

4 tbsp olive oil

2 cups water

Directions:

Heat the oil in a large skillet and cook the onions and the carrot until soft. Add the paprika and the washed and drained rice and stir to combine.

Add two cups of warm water stirring constantly as the rice absorbs it, and simmer for 10 more minutes.

Wash the spinach well and cut it in strips then add to the rice and cook until it wilts. Remove from the heat and season to taste.

Vegetable Stew

Serves 6-7

Ingredients:

3-4 potatoes, peeled and diced

2-3 tomatoes, diced

1-2 carrots, chopped

1-2 onions, finely chopped

1 zucchini, chopped

1 eggplant, chopped

1 celery rib, chopped

½ cup green peas, frozen

½ green beans, frozen

4 tbsp sunflower oil

1 bunch of parsley

1 tsp black pepper

1/2 tsp salt

Directions:

Sauté the finely chopped onions, carrots and celery in a little oil. Add the green peas, the green beans, black pepper and stir well.

Pour over 1 cup of water, cover and let simmer. After 15 minutes add the diced potatoes, the zucchini, eggplant and tomato pieces.

Transfer everything into a clay pot, sprinkle with parsley and bake for about 30 minutes at 350 F.

Simple Baked Beans

Serves 8-10

Ingredients:

1 ½ cup dried white beans

2 medium onions

1 red bell pepper, chopped

1 carrot, chopped

1/4 cup sunflower oil

1 tbsp paprika

1 tsp black pepper

½ bunch fresh parsley

7-8 fresh mint leaves mint

1 tsp salt

Directions:

Wash the beans and soak them in water overnight. In the morning discard the water, pour enough cold water to cover the beans, add one of the onions, peeled but left whole.

Bring to the boil and simmer until the beans are soft but not falling apart. If there is too much water left, drain the beans.

Chop the second onion and sauté it in a frying pan along with the chopped bell pepper and the carrot. Add paprika and the beans. Stir well and pour the mixture in a baking dish along with some parsley, mint, and salt.

Bake in a preheated to 350 F oven for 20-30 minutes. The beans should not be too dry. Serve warm.

Rice Stuffed Bell Peppers

Serves 4

Ingredients:

8 bell peppers, cored and seeded

1½ cups rice

2 onions, chopped

1 tomato, chopped

1/2 cup fresh parsley, chopped

3 tbsp olive oil

1 tbsp paprika

Directions:

Heat the oil and sauté the onions for 2-3 minutes. Add the paprika, the washed and rinsed rice, the tomato, and season with salt and pepper. Add ½ cup of hot water and cook the rice until the water is absorbed.

Stuff each pepper with the mixture using a spoon. Every pepper should be ¾ full.

Arrange the peppers in a deep oven proof dish and top up with warm water to half fill the dish. Cover and bake for about 20 minutes at 350 F.

Uncover and cook for another 15 minutes until the peppers are well cooked.

Stuffed Red Bell Peppers with Haricot Beans

Serves 5

Ingredients:

10 dried red bell peppers

1 cup dried white beans

1 onion

3 cloves garlic, cut

1 carrot, chopped

1 bunch of parsley

½ cup crushed walnuts

1 tsp paprika

salt, to taste

Directions:

Put the dried peppers in warm water and leave them for 1 hour.

Cook the beans and drain the water.

Chop the carrot and the onion, sauté them and add them to the cooked beans. Add as well the finely chopped parsley and the walnuts. Stir the mixture to combine everything well.

Drain the peppers, then fill them with the mixture and place in a ovenproof baking dish. Bake for about 30 minutes at 350 F.

Stuffed Grapevine Leaves

Serves 6-7

Ingredients:

1.5 oz grapevine leaves, canned

2 cups rice

2 onions, chopped

2-3 cloves garlic, chopped

½ cup of currants

half bunch of parsley

half bunch of dill

1 lemon, juice only

1 tsp dried mint

1 tsp salt

1 tsp black pepper

1/4 cup olive oil

Directions:

Heat 3 tablespoons of olive oil in a frying pan and sauté the onions and garlic until golden. Add the washed and drained rice, the currants, dill and parsley. Add the remaining olive oil and the juice of one lemon. Stir in black pepper, dried mint and salt.

Place a leaf on a chopping board, with the stalk towards you and the vein side up. Snip away any tough remnants of the vein. Place about 1 teaspoon of the filling in the center of the leaf and towards the bottom edge.

Fold the bottom part of the leaf over the filling, then draw the sides in and towards the middle, rolling the leaf up. The vine leaves should be well tucked in, forming a neat parcel. The stuffing should feel compact and evenly distributed.

Cover the bottom of a pot with grapevine leaves and arrange the stuffed vine leaf parcels, packing them tightly together, on top. Pour some water, to just below the level of the stuffed leaves. Place a small, flat ovenproof dish upside down on top, in order to prevent scattering.

Cover with a lid. Bring to the boil, then reduce the heat and simmer for about an hour checking occasionally that the bottom of the pot does not burn. Serve warm or cold.

Green Bean and Potato Stew

Serves 5-6

Ingredients:

2 cups green beans, fresh or frozen

2 onions, chopped

4 cloves garlic, crushed

1/3 cup olive oil

1 cup fresh parsley, chopped

1 bunch of fresh dill, finely chopped

3-4 potatoes, peeled and cut in small chunks

2 carrots, sliced

½ cup water

2 tsp tomato paste

salt and pepper, to taste

Directions:

Gently sauté the onions and garlic in olive oil. Add the green beans and all remaining ingredients.

Cover and simmer over medium heat for about 40 minutes, or until all vegetables are tender.

Check after 30 minutes; add more water if necessary. Serve warm-sprinkled with fresh dill.

Cabbage and Rice Stew

Serves 4

Ingredients:

1 cup long grain white rice

2 cups water

2 tbsp olive oil

1 small onion, chopped

1 clove garlic, crushed

1/2 head cabbage, cored and shredded

2 tomatoes, diced

1 tbsp paprika

1 tsp cumin

½ bunch of parsley, finely cut

salt, to taste

black pepper, to taste

Directions:

Heat the olive oil in a large pot. Add the onion and garlic and cook until transparent. Add paprika, cumin, rice and water, stir, and bring to a boil.

Simmer for 10 minutes. Add the shredded cabbage, tomatoes, and cook for about 20 minutes, stirring occasionally, until the cabbage cooks down.

Season with salt and pepper and serve sprinkled with fresh parsley.

Rice with Leeks and Olives

Serves 4-6

Ingredients:

6 large leeks, cleaned and sliced into bite sized pieces (about 6-7 cups of sliced leeks)

1 large onion, chopped

20 black olives pitted, chopped

½ cup hot water

4-5 tbsp olive oil

1 cup rice

2 cups boiling water

freshly-ground black pepper, to taste

Directions:

In a large saucepan, sauté the leeks and onion in olive oil for 4-5 minutes. Cut and add the olives and ½ cup water.

Bring temperature down, cover saucepan and cook for 10 minutes, stirring occasionally.

Add rice and 2 cups of hot water, bring to a boil, cover and simmer for 15 more minutes, stirring occasionally.

Remove from heat and set aside for 15 minutes before serving so that the rice can absorb any liquid left.

Rice and Tomatoes

Serves 6-7

Ingredients:

1 cup rice

1 large onion, chopped

1 tbsp paprika

5 tbsp cup olive oil

1 tsp summer savory

2 cups canned tomatoes, diced, or 5 big ripe tomatoes

½ bunch fresh parsley, finely cut

1 tsp sugar

Directions:

Wash and drain the rice. In a large saucepan, sauté the onion in olive oil for 4-5 minutes. Add paprika and rice and cook, stirring constantly, until the rice becomes transparent.

Pour 2 cups of hot water and the tomatoes. Mix well and season with salt, pepper, summer savory and a tsp of sugar to neutralize the acidic taste of the tomatoes.

Simmer over medium heath for about 20 minutes. When ready sprinkle with parsley and serve.

Roasted Cauliflower

Serves 4

Ingredients:

1 medium cauliflower, cut into bite sized pieces

4 garlic cloves, lightly crushed

4-5 fresh rosemary leaves, finely cut

salt, to taste

black pepper, to taste

1/4 cup olive oil

Directions:

Mix oil, rosemary, salt, pepper and garlic together. Toss in cauliflower and place in a baking dish in one layer.

Roast in a preheated oven at 350 F for 20 minutes; stir and bake for 10 more minutes.

Stuffed Cabbage Leaves

Serves 8

Ingredients:

20-30 pickled cabbage leaves

1 onion, chopped

2 leeks stems, chopped

1½ cup white rice

½ cup currants

½ cup almonds, blanched, peeled, and chopped

2 tsp paprika

1 tbsp dried mint

½ tsp black pepper

½ cup olive oil

salt, to taste

Directions:

Sauté the onion and the leeks in the oil for about 2-3 minutes. Add paprika, black pepper and the washed and drained rice and continue sautéing until the rice is translucent.

Remove from heat and add the currants, finely chopped almonds and the peppermint. Add salt only if the cabbage leaves are not too salty.

In a large pot, place a few cabbage leaves on the base. Place a cabbage leaf on a large plate with the thickest part closest to you. Spoon 1-2 teaspoons of the rice mixture and fold over each edge to create a tight sausage-like parcel.

Place in the pot, making two or three layers. Cover with a few cabbage leaves and pour over some boiling water so that the water level remains lower than the top layer of cabbage leaves. Top with a small dish upside down to prevent scattering.

Bring to the boil then lower the heat and cook for about 40 minutes. Serve warm or at room temperature.

Potato and Zucchini Bake

Serves 6

Ingredients:

1½ lb potatoes, peeled and sliced into rounds

5 zucchinis, sliced into rounds

2 onions, sliced into rounds

3 tomatoes, pureed

½ cup water

4 tbsp olive oil

1 tsp dry oregano

1/3 cup fresh parsley leaves, chopped

salt and black pepper, to taste

Directions:

Place the potatoes, zucchinis and onions in a large, shallow ovenproof baking dish. Pour over the the olive oil and pureed tomatoes. Add salt and freshly ground pepper to taste and toss the everything together. Add in the water.

Bake in a preheated to 350 F oven for an hour, stirring halfway through.

New Potatoes with Herbs

Serves 4-5

Ingredients:

2.25 oz small new potatoes

1 tbsp mint

5 tbsp olive oil

1/3 cup finely chopped parsley

6-7 fresh rosemary leaves, chopped

4-5 fresh oregano leaves

1 tbsp dill, chopped

1 tsp salt

1 tsp black pepper

Directions:

Wash the young potatoes, cut them in halves if too big, and put them in a baking dish. Pour over the olive oil.

Season with the herbs, salt and pepper. Bake for 30-40 minutes at 350 F.

Okra and Tomato Casserole

Serves 4-5

Ingredients:

1 lb okra, stem ends trimmed

4 large tomatoes, cut into wedges

3 garlic cloves, chopped

3 tbsp olive oil

1 tsp salt

black pepper, to taste

Directions:

In a large casserole, mix together trimmed okra, sliced tomatoes, olive oil and the chopped garlic. Add salt and pepper and toss to combine.

Bake in a preheated to 350 F oven for 45 minutes, or until the okra is tender.

Roasted Brussels Sprouts

Serves 4-5

Ingredients:

1 ½ lb Brussels sprouts, rinsed

1 tbsp summer savory

3 tbsp olive oil

3 tbsp balsamic vinegar

salt and black pepper, to taste

Directions:

Preheat the oven to 400 F. Place whole sprouts in a medium bowl. (If they are too large-cut in half). Add olive oil, balsamic vinegar and and summer savory and toss. Season with salt and pepper.

Layer sprouts on a baking sheet and roast for 35 minutes, stirring a couple of times, or until tender. Serve warm.

Roasted Butternut Squash

Serves 4

Ingredients:

½ butternut squash, peeled, seeds removed, flesh chopped

2 sprigs fresh rosemary, leaves only

2 garlic cloves, finely chopped

3-4 tbsp olive oil

salt and freshly ground black pepper

Directions:

Preheat the oven to 350 F. Place the butternut squash pieces onto a baking tray and scatter over the rosemary and the chopped garlic. Drizzle with olive oil and season, to taste, with salt and freshly ground black pepper.

Transfer to the oven and roast for 12-15 minutes, or until the squash is tender and golden-brown.

Roasted Artichoke Hearts

Serves 4

Ingredients:

2 cans artichoke hearts

4 garlic cloves, quartered

2 tbsp olive oil

1 tsp summer savory

salt and pepper, to taste

2-3 tbsp lemon juice, to serve

Directions:

Preheat oven to 350 F. Drain artichokes hearts and rinse them well. Place them in a bowl and toss in garlic, savory and olive oil.

Pour artichoke mixture in a baking dish and bake for about 45 minutes tossing a few times if desired. Season with salt and pepper, and serve with lemon juice.

Beet Fries

Serves 4

Ingredients:

3 red beets, cut in strips

3 tbsp olive oil

a bunch of spring onions, finely cut

2 cloves of garlic, crushed

1 tsp salt

Directions:

Line a baking dish with baking paper. Wash and peel beets then cut them in strips similar to French fries. Toss the beets with the olive oil, spring onions, garlic and salt.

Arrange the beet fries on a prepared baking sheet and place in a preheated to 425 F oven for 25-30 minutes, flipping halfway through.

Grilled Vegetable Skewers

Serves 4

Ingredients:

1 red pepper

1 green pepper

3 zucchinis, halved lengthwise and sliced

3 onions, quartered

12 medium mushrooms, whole

2 garlic cloves, crushed

1 tsp summer savory

1 tsp cumin

1 spring fresh rosemary, leaves only

salt and ground black pepper

2 tbsp olive oil

Directions:

Deseed and cut the peppers into chunks. Divide between 6 skewers threading alternately with the zucchinis, onions and mushrooms. Set aside the skewers in a shallow plate.

Mix the crushed garlic with the herbs, cumin, salt, black pepper and olive oil. Roll each skewer in the mixture.

Bake them on a hot barbecue or char grill, turning occasionally, until slightly charred.

Vegan Gluten-free Breakfasts and Desserts

Quinoa Banana Pudding

Serves 4

Ingredients:

1 cup quinoa

2 cups water

3 ripe bananas

4 cups water

4 tbsp sugar

1 tsp vanilla extract

Directions:

Wash and cook quinoa according to package directions. When ready remove from heat and set aside.

In a separate bowl blend sugar and bananas until smooth. Add to the quinoa. Heat over medium heat, string until creamy. Stir in vanilla and serve warm.

Raisin Quinoa Breakfast

Serves 2

Ingredients:

½ cup quinoa

1 cup water

1 tsp cinnamon

½ tsp vanilla

½ tsp ground flax seed

2 tbsp walnuts or almonds, chopped

2 tbsp raisins

3-4 tbsp pure maple syrup

Directions:

Rinse quinoa and drain. Place water and quinoa into a small saucepan and bring to a boil. Add cinnamon and vanilla.

Reduce heat to low and simmer for about 15 minutes stirring often.

When ready, place a portion of the quinoa into a bowl, drizzle with maple syrup and top with flax seeds, raisins and crushed walnuts.

Berry Quinoa Breakfast

Serves 2

Ingredients:

½ cup quinoa

1 cup water

¼ cup fresh blueberries or raspberries

1 tbsp walnuts or almonds, chopped

3-4 tbsp pure maple syrup

1 tbsp chia seeds

Directions:

Wash quinoa and cook according to package directions.

When ready, add walnuts and cinnamon, place a portion of the quinoa into a bowl and top with fresh blueberries, chia seeds and maple syrup.

Baked Apples

Serves 4

Ingredients:

8 medium sized apples

1/3 cup walnuts, crushed

3/4 cup sugar

3 tbsp raisins, soaked

vanilla, cinnamon according to taste

Directions:

Peel and carefully hollow the apples.

Prepare the stuffing by mixing 3/4 cup of sugar, crushed walnuts, raisins and cinnamon.

Stuff the apples and place them in an oiled dish. Pour over 1-2 tbsp of water and bake in a moderate oven. Serve warm.

Pumpkin Baked with Dry Fruit

Serves 5-6

Ingredients:

1.5 lb pumpkin, cut into medium pieces

1 cup dry fruit (apricots, plums, apples, raisins)

½ cup brown sugar

Directions:

Soak the dry fruit in some water, drain and discard the water.

Cut the pumpkin in medium cubes. At the bottom of a pot arrange a layer of pumpkin pieces, then a layer of dry fruit and then again some pumpkin. Add a little water.

Cover the pot and bring to boil. Simmer until there is no more water left. When almost ready add the sugar. Serve warm or cold.

About the Author

Vesela lives in Bulgaria with her family of six (including the Jack Russell Terrier). Her passion is going green in everyday life and she loves to prepare homemade cosmetic and beauty products for all her family and friends.

Vesela has been publishing her cookbooks for over a year now. If you want to see other healthy family recipes that she has published, together with some natural beauty books, you can check out her [Author Page](#) on Amazon.

Printed in Great Britain
by Amazon